بِسْمِ اللهِ الرَّحْمٰنِ الرَّحِيمِ

ADVICE

TO OUR BROTHERS
THE SCHOLARS OF

NAJD

ADVICE
TO OUR BROTHERS
THE SCHOLARS OF
NAJD

Sayyid
Yusuf Hashim al-Rifaʻi

Introduction by
Shaykh Muhammad Saʻid al-Buti

Translation and notes
Gibril Fouad Haddad

Foreword by
Asrar Rashid

TAFTAZANI PRESS
INSTITUTE FOR SPIRITUAL & CULTURAL ADVANCEMENT

Nasihah li Ikhwanina 'Ulama' Najd
Advice to our Brothers the Scholars of Najd

Written by Sayyid Yusuf Hashim al-Rifa'i
Translation & notes by Gibril Fouad Haddad

ISBN (Taftazani Press): 979-8-324132-88-0
ISBN (Institute for Spiritual and Cultural Advancement): 978-1-938058-76-9

June 2024 / Dhu al-Qa'dah 1445

Book design, editing and typesetting by Ibrahim Hussain

Cover design by Ramy Najmeddine

Special thanks to Sultaan Khalid

Sayyid Yusuf Hashim al-Rifa'i flanked by
Gibril Fouad Haddad and Asrar Rashid (*picture right*)
and by Abd al-Shukor Hadi and Abu 'Imran (*picture left*)
in Damascus, 2002.

CONTENTS

Foreword

by *Asrar Rashid*

The movement of Ibn 'Abd al-Wahhab in the 1700s was the cause of major disruption and violence amongst Muslims. Towns such as Ta'if, Ahsa', Karbala' and surrounding regions of Najd were ransacked and thousands of Muslims were killed under the pretext of being *mushrikīn*.[1]

This led to the formation of the first Saudi kingdom.[2] Subsequently, in the early 1800s, the Ottoman Sultan[3] decimated the first Saudi kingdom. Later on, in the mid-1800s, a second Saudi kingdom was established which also was later vanquished in around 1902. The third Saudi kingdom was established, which after the formal abolition of the Ottoman Caliphate in 1924, seized the holy cities of Makkah and Madina, not for the first time, as they had done so in the past during the existence of the first Saudi Kingdom.

The establishment of the third Saudi kingdom coincided with the discovery of oil fields in the Arabian Peninsula in the 1930s and the introduction of printing houses across the Middle East. This affluence led many rich Najdi businessmen to fund and finance the growth of the Najdi literature, reprinting the works of Muhammad ibn 'Abd al-Wahhab and anyone aligned to his ideology. This went hand in hand with the likes of Rashid Rida,[4] in Egypt, in the early 1900s republishing many works that were formerly unknown amongst the Sunni masses containing Najdi ideology.

[1] In his history work *Tarīkh Najd*, Ibn 'Abd al-Wahhab's own student, Husayn ibn Ghannam documented approximately 317 areas that were excommunicated and subsequently fought and massacred.

[2] The Emirate of Diriyah that was formed between Ibn 'Abd al-Wahhab and Muhammad ibn Saud.

[3] Sultan Mahmud II.

[4] See Hüseyn Hilmi Işık's comprehensive refutations of Rashid Rida titled *Answer to an Enemy of Islam* and *Islam's Reformers*.

The foundation of Najdi ideology in claiming Sunni Muslims to be *mushrikīn* is based upon their definition of *tawḥīd* and polytheism (*shirk*). The Najdis believe that the polytheists of Makkah were familiar with *tawḥīd* in terms of acknowledging that Allah alone is the creator, sustainer and controller of all matters. The only distinction was that the polytheists worshipped other gods alongside Allah.

The Sunni definition of *shirk*, distinct to the Najdi definition, is ascribing divinity to the essence (*dhāt*) of other than Allah or ascribing divine attributes (*sifāt*) to other than Allah or divine actions (*afʿāl*) to other than Allah. The Najdis, on the other hand, claim that a person can have *tawḥīd* in lordship (*rubūbiyyah*) by acknowledging Allah alone as the creator but simultaneously violate the essentials of *tawhid* by worshipping other than Allah.

The Sunnis make a distinction between *shirk* and disbelief (*kufr*), in terms of all *shirk* is *kufr* but not all *kufr* is *shirk*. So a person can become a *kafir* through blasphemy but not necessarily *shirk*. *Shirk* is only committed when the person ascribes divinity or divine attributes or divine actions to other than Allah. Therefore seeking help (*istighāthah*) through the Messenger of Allah ﷺ by a Muslim is never *shirk* because the Muslim does not ascribe divinity, divine attributes or divine actions to the Prophet ﷺ.

The Najdis however made a distinction of *istighāthah* through the Prophet ﷺ while he was alive on earth and after he passed away. They deemed it permissible when he was alive on earth and permissible on the Day of Judgement but impermissible and *shirk* after he had passed away on earth. The Sunnis countered this by establishing the mass-transmitted *hadīth* (*mutawātir*) that the Prophet ﷺ, after tasting death, is alive in the grave by Allah having returned his soul back to his body and the bodies of the prophets are preserved and they also worship in their graves and supplicate for their nations.[5] The Sunnis also established the fact that the actions of the nation (*ummah*) of the Prophet ﷺ are presented to him in his grave and he supplicates for them,[6] and this is the essence of *tawassul* and *istighāthah*.

The Najdis, being unable to comprehend this, claim that such a concept is *shirk* because the Sunnis have ascribed divinity to the Prophet ﷺ. The Sunnis respond to this by making clear distinction between the divine attributes of Allah, namely being all hearing and all seeing, and the fact that Allah enables the Prophet ﷺ and creates for him the ability to see the actions of his nation from the grave. The clear distinction being that divine attributes are eternal (*qadīm*) while created attributes are contingent (*hādith*).

In addition to this, the Sunnis presented verses of the Qur'an and many *ahadith* to validate their claim as well as the statements of *'ulamā* across the centuries. The Najdis, in response, reinterpreted many verses of the Qur'an in accordance with the ideas of Ibn Taymiyyah[7] and claimed that the *ahadith* cited by the Sunnis were weak.

Despite all of the 'logical' reasoning and inconsistent definitions of *tawhīd* and *shirk* by the Najdi movement, they were still unable to make a distinction between actions which could be deemed *harām*, *makrūh tahrīman*, *mubāh*, *mustahhab* and would simply label all of these things as *shirk*.

---

[5] The *ahadith* are so many in number that they cannot all be mentioned here, see al-Maliki's *The Life of the Prophets in Their Graves* for documentation of these sound narrations.

[6] Ibn Mas'ud narrates that the Prophet ﷺ said: "My life is an immense good for you: you bring up new matters and new matters are brought up for you. My death, also, is an immense good for you: your actions will be shown to me; if I see goodness I shall praise Allah and if I see evil I shall ask forgiveness of Him for you.." (*al-Bazzar*)

[7] See '*Ahmad ibn Taymiyya (661-728)*' by Shaykh Gibril Fouad Haddad

What compounded the belligerent behaviour and dialectic of Ibn 'Abd al-Wahhab and his epigones was the *madhāhir al-ghulūw* (behaviours of exaggeration) towards certain shrines and the use of metaphorical language when calling upon the *Awliyā'*. In reality, these issues are issues of *fiqh* which the *fuqahā* discussed in the works of the four Sunni *madhāhib*.

For instance, kissing the grave of a pious person is deemed permissible by some Hanbalis but impermissible by some Hanafis and even disputed amongst them. The Hanbalis give a citation from Imam Ahmad bin Hanbal who permitted kissing the *mimbar* of the Prophet ﷺ and such similar examples.

On the other hand, the Hanafis who prohibit the kissing of graves, like Imam Ahmad Rida al-Barelwi[8] give the reasoning of preventing the general public from carrying out such types of actions because they lead to more erroneous acts and also because a person should maintain complete *adab* when visiting the Prophet ﷺ and not shout and raise their voice or embrace the walls of the chamber (*hujrah*) or kiss the blessed grave.

This is a similar case to that of a person who does *istighāthah* (seeking help) from other than Allah whilst believing that Allah creates the ability to help within the one sought after for help and not ascribing divinity or divine attributes/actions to the one being sought for help. This then becomes an issue of *fiqh* and not an issue of *'aqīdah*.

Thus if a Muslim calls upon a *walī* for *madad* (assistance) believing the *walī's* spirit (*rūh*) has *tasarruf* and ability to intervene and intercede to Allah, this Muslim is not deemed as a *mushrik*. This is again due to the fact that he does not ascribe divinity or divine attributes/actions to the *walī*.

[8] See *al-Zubdah al-Zakiyyah li-Tahreem Sujood al-Tahiyyah* of Imam Ahmad Rida al-Barelwi

However, whether this action is deemed as *haram* or permissible is actually an issue of *fiqh* and not an issue of *'aqīdah*.

Therefore, some jurists have said this is impermissible like Zayn al-Din al-Iraqi in the Shafi'ii school based upon the wordings of the common people which could be misconstrued as being an ascription of divinity or divine attributes or divine actions to other than Allah.

On the other hand, other jurists in the Shafi'i school permitted this form of *istighāthah* through a *walī* like Ibn Hajar al-Haytami al-Makki, Shaykh al-Islam Zakariyyah al-Ansari and a host of others.

As for *istighāthah* through the Prophet ﷺ specifically, then this is deemed permissible by the overwhelming majority of jurists in all four *madhāhib* as it was permissible in the worldly life of the Prophet ﷺ just as it will be permissible on the Day of Judgement and can never be deemed *shirk* because an action of *shirk* always remains as such.

These theological predilections held by the Najdi *'ulama* and the Saudi government, led to policies within the *Hijāz* of destruction of many holy sites and the destruction of the *Qubab* (domes) surrounding many historical graves including the graves of Sayyidah Fatimah, al-Imam al-Hasan, Sayyiduna 'Uthman and many other *sahābah* (may Allah be well-pleased with them all) and Imams like Imam Malik in the graveyard of *al-Baqi*. This was based on the Najdi position that these graves were deemed as *asnām* (idols) and the destruction of these idols was essential to purify the land from polytheism (*shirk*). Citation was also given to some of the *athār*, reported from the likes of Sayyiduna 'Ali (may Allah be well-pleased with him), that Rasulallah ﷺ had despatched people to destroy graves that were raised above the ground, above an arms length.

5

Therefore, the Najdi justification for destruction of those sites was based upon the *istighāthah* of the common people, calling upon those *sahābah* or *awliyā'* buried in those graves and the belief that those buried in those graves were a *sabab* (means) to *shirk*. This coincided with the destruction of the old Ottoman Caliphate infrastructure and replacing it with Western-style infrastructure and corporations. On top of historical sights, towers were constructed with corporations like McDonalds and KFC and hotels belonging to private individuals in the western world, to profiteer from the *Hajj* and *'Umrah* of the Muslims. Therefore, whilst they perform *Hajj* and *'Umrah*, the Muslims would not know of the historical relevance of the graveyard of *al-Ma'la* in Makkah or the graveyard of *al-Baqi* and the location of the graves of major *sahābah*, *Ahl al-Bayt* and Imams of this *Ummah* but rather they were encouraged to shop in large shopping malls and to purchase Western products in order to increase capitalisation profiteering for the Saudi government and its Western high-tech north allies.

Of course, the claim that constructing a room around a grave is prohibited actually has no basis in understanding the *fiqh* of the *hadīth* for indeed the Prophet ﷺ himself was buried in the chamber of Sayyidah 'Aishah (may Allah be well-pleased with her). Some of the Najdi callers claim that this was specific to the Prophet ﷺ but this is contradicted by the fact that Sayyiduna Abu Bakr al Siddiq and Sayyiduna 'Umar (may Allah be well-pleased with them), who were the first two Caliphs and successors of the Prophet ﷺ in governance, were also buried in the chamber of Sayyidah 'Aisha (may Allah be well-pleased with her). A chamber which surrounded the graves and also had a roof. There is no difference between a dome structure and a flat roof except that one is curved and the other is flat.

Therefore, constructing four walls around the grave of a notable person and a roof, firstly preserves the grave itself from destruction, like what some of the *Rafidis* intend to do with some of the graves of the *sahābah* or what some of the Najdis attempt to do with the graves of the *sahābah*. An example is what occurred in Libya during the so called 'Arab Spring', which in reality was an Arab winter, during which they destroyed the grave of a particular *sahabī*[9] in Libya and exhumed the body of Sidi Ahmad Zarruq in Libya also. So four walls around a grave preserves the grave and also stops the lay-people from touching the actual grave, from performing *sajdah* to the grave, from accessing the grave and carrying out acts deemed as extreme acts. Extreme acts such as bowing to the grave or *sajdah* to the grave or circumambulating the grave. It also gives the benefit of preserving those historical sights so that future generations will know where the graves of certain *sahabah* exist.

Many Najdi youth are uninformed regarding the recommendation of the Prophet ﷺ for people to visit graves. This command of the Prophet ﷺ abrogated previous prohibitions of visiting graves and many of the *sahābah* would visit graves because visitation of the graves not only reminds a person of the *ākhirah* and the short-lived nature of this *dunya* but also creates a deep connection with our *salaf* (pious predecessors) and our Islamic roots, heritage and history.

The result of the Najdi movement within Saudi Arabia today is visible; that people who have become disconnected with their Islamic roots now choose atheism or secularism as an alternative way of life. The trajectory to the way of atheism in Arabia is different to the trajectory taken by the Turks. Turkish atheism was based upon Atatürk's enforcement of secularisation as well as his persecution and killing of *'ulama* but Turkey still preserved its islamic heritage and sights in terms of the preservation of the graves of the righteous, the historical architecture and *masājid*. This means that when Turkish youth return back to Islam, they will be able to find a physical embodiment of their Islamic history which affects the psyche and spirituality of a person. This is unlike the policies of the Najdi Saudi regime

---

[9] The grave being referred to is the grave of Sayyiduna Zuhayr ibn Qays al-Balawi (may Allah be well-pleased with him).

which destroyed most of the vestiges and historical sights, or barred people from visiting the place of Badr in the past, meaning that people could not visit the site of a historical battle against *shirk* and *kufr*, which established the *dīn* of Islam within the Arabian Peninsula.

Today there are many youths brainwashed by the pseudo-Salafi Najdi ideology and it takes many forms. From the form of the *Madkhalī* brand, which calls for total obedience to leaders who may go as far as to recognise the entity of 'Israel' despite its genocide in Gaza and at the same time they condemn any resistance against that genocide. On the other hand, you may have Najdis who are pro-Palestine and against the regimes but deem the Sunni Sufi *Ash'aris* as being *mushrikin* (polytheists) that are unclean and when these types of people take power in any part of the muslim world they attempt to eradicate and kill Sunni Muslims.

This is unlike the true Sunni muslims who held sway over the Caliphate for the majority of the time, with the odd exception of when the *Mu'tazilites* held sway. However, the Sunni Muslims for the most part, with the odd exceptions, allowed the various schools and sects to live in peace, even though our Sunni theologians, the *Ash'ari mutakallimīn*, destroyed their arguments on a textual and rational basis.

Among those prominent *Ash'ari 'ulamā* was Shaykh Sayyid Yusuf al-Rifa'i, the author of this book which was written as a reminder to the *'ulama* of Najd. A reminder that they must give up their excesses in their wanton destruction of Islamic heritage and labelling Muslims as *mushrikīn*. This book was translated by Dr. Gibril Fouad Haddad in Damascus, wherein he resided and studied under major *'ulama* there. The likes of Shaykh Nur al-Din 'Itr, Shaykh Adib Kallas, Shaykh Muhammad Sa'id Ramadan al-Buti and innumerable other *'ulamā* and he also received *ijazat* in the sciences of *hadīth*.

The book has an introduction of a great 'Alim of Islam, misunderstood by many for his position in 2010 with regard to the Syrian uprising against the tyrant Bashar al-Assad. Shaykh Muhammad Sa'id Ramadan al-Buti did not defend tyranny and oppression but was rather safeguarding the blood of hundreds of thousands of Muslims within Syria. Of course, this short introduction is not the place to discuss the historical events of the Syrian uprising and the tyranny of any of the regimes in the majority Muslim countries but we ask Allah to bring about a *sultān ʿādil* (just ruler) to bring about balance on the Earth.

We hope that this book benefits many of the younger people who have been brainwashed by the pseudo-Salafi Najdi ideology and have adopted abandonment of the four *madhāhib*, claiming to do *ijtihād* directly from the books of the Sunnah for which they do not have the requisite tools and also falsely claiming that having attachment to the *awliyā'* entails *shirk* and *bidʿah*.

Asrar Rashid
Birmingham, United Kingdom
5 Dhu al-Qaʾdah 1445 AH
13 May 2024 CE

Introduction:

The *Salaf* Loved the Prophet ﷺ and Preserved His Vestiges and So Should our Brothers of Najd

Shaykh Dr. Muhammad Saʿid Ramadan al-Buti

All praise belongs to Allah Most High, by Whose favour good deeds become accomplished! Blessings and greeting upon our Master Muhammad and upon his Family and all his Companions!

To proceed: Sayyid Yusuf al-Rifaʿi is one of the most remarkable, eminent personalities and scholars of Kuwait. He has brought together in his knowledge of Islam, ever since I have known him, scholarly endeavor with the call to Islam as well as humanitarian and social efforts and works of charity. He has always been commanding good and forbidding evil as much as possible, his reliance in this being – after knowledge – his love for the sake of Allah and his concern for the servants of Allah . He has kept contact with all the Muslims regardless of their different groups and communities, the way a brother keeps in touch with his Muslim brethren always striving to reform the latter by extending the bridges of mutual sincere advice to them. In this he took for his guide the Divine command **Therefore make peace between your brethren** (49:10) and the directive of the Messenger of Allah ﷺ who said: "Religion is sincere, faithful advice..."

Such is the sign of the truthful among the servants of Allah and those who are sincere in putting His commands into effect and truly following His precepts. We detect and recognize them thus, without presuming anything on the part of Allah.

I read this epistle of his. All it took to make me read it was its title that shines with the marks of appreciation for others, purity of purpose, and the motivation of cooperation in the way of seeking Divine good pleasure:

Advice to Our Brothers the Scholars of Najd. Had I seen something contrary to these elements in the title I would not have paid any attention to the book nor wasted dearly precious time reading it.

When I began to read it I saw exactly what conformed with the promise of the title and fulfilled it: a quiet, kind reminder and counsels that show true jealous concern over the Religion of Allah as well as pure concern for those brethren lest they stray from the path of Allah.

I reviewed the counsels of my brother, Sayyid Yusuf al-Rifaʿi, to those brothers from the first to the last. Then I weighed those counsels in the scales of the Divine Law as I understand them to be, its proofs, and its source-texts. I found him in the right in all of his advices and warnings to them. More than that, he is truly speaking, in this capacity, in the name of all the Ulema of the Muslims who follow the guidance of the Qur'an and Sunna and tread the path and method of the pious Predecessors, whoever and wherever they are.

I truly do not know if the Islamic World ever concurred in its indignation over a single matter in its entire history the way it does today over what is being perpetrated by the brethren who are in charge of the Kingdom [of Saudi Arabia] **and by its scholars in the evisceration of Makka and Madina and their vicinities of all the historical remnants connected with the life of the Messenger of Allah** صلى الله عليه وسلم **– both as a private person and as a prophet – and, subsequently, their perpetrating deeds that violate Islamic Law and violate the method which the pious Predecessors (*al-Salaf al-Sâlih*) used to apply.** Namely: prohibiting the Muslims from visiting al-Baqiʿ, prohibiting them from being buried in it, and declaring the larger mass of this Community apostates on the pretext that they are Ashʿaris or Maturidis! And was Imam al-Ashʿari anything but the defender of the pious Predecessors by the Consensus of the Community of Islam?!

What adds to this indignation which, today, has reached its climax is the fact that those brethren who are committing these abominations persist in their way and continue doing so in the midst of silence and general indifference! But the least degree of conformity to the priorities of the Religion of Islam and the most obvious, agreed-upon basics in its rulings require them to begin, first, by publishing an open statement in the plain sight and hearing of the Islamic World in which they show the proof for what, in their opinion, constitutes the obligation of destroying and eradicating from the face of the earth the historical remnants of Prophethood whatever they are and wherever they are found.

Thereafter, they would have been required to announce their decision – on the bases mentioned above – to go ahead and put into effect the stipulations of the legal ruling paired with its proof.

I was and continue to be but one of millions of Muslims who are astonished at what is presently going on in Makka and Madina, right under the eyes of the Muslims from the Eastern reaches of the earth to the farthest West, with the flippant dismissal of their symbols, their knowledge and learning, and their beliefs. All this takes place without the slightest excuse being offered before they venture into those strange affairs: not one scholarly argument to which they might cling, nor one example of juridical exertion (*ijtihâd*) to which they might rightfully refer.

I even preferred, in my amazement, to begin by blaming myself for my ignorance. I thought there was probably something wrong in my information which I mistakenly took for right, or some legal ruling of which I was unaware. I thought this in conformity with our obligation to keep a good opinion of our Muslim brethren – especially the scholars among them – as much as possible. So I went back and dug up the biographies of the pious Predecessors and looked up their position. I began with the time of the

Companions then the following periods to find out anew precisely where they stood from the use of relics and the historical vestiges of Prophethood – whether the personal relics of the Messenger of Allah or those vestiges connected to his Message and Prophethood. **I found nothing but Consensus (ijmâ') – beginning with the time of the Messenger of Allah ﷺ – on the lawfulness of seeking blessing through his relics.** More than that, I saw that all of the Companions raced and competed in such pursuit. **And there is no doubt that the Shaykhs of Najd know what we all know of the existence of rigorously authentic and firmly established narrations in the two books of Sahih** [al-Bukhari and Muslim] **and in other books, to the effect that the Companions derived blessings from the sweat of the Messenger of Allah ﷺ, his hair, the water he used for ablution, his saliva, the cup he drank in, and the spots in which he prayed, sat, or napped.**

Nor do we doubt that they know, just as we know, that the three time-periods of the Predecessors stand witness in consensus to the practice of deriving blessings from the historical remnants by which they remembered the Messenger of Allah ﷺ. For example, the house of his birth; the house of Khadija – may Allah be well-pleased with her!; the house of Abu Ayyub al-Ansari (may Allah be well pleased with him) which first welcomed him and in which he resided in the first day of his Migration to Madina the Radiant; and others of the vestiges such as the well of Aris, the well of Dhu Tuwa, the house of Arqam... Then the generations that succeeded followed in the same steps and were the best guardians of these relics and a dependable witness to the abovementioned Consensus.

In our time, the Islamic World in its entirety is shocked by this innovation with which our brethren, the Shaykhs of Najd, are tearing apart the Consensus of the Predecessors of the Muslims and their Successors to our day. **The house that saw the birth of the Messenger of Allah ﷺ was razed and transformed into a cattle market and the house that**

was the first home of the Messenger of Allah ﷺ in Madina was changed into latrines!

And so do the hands of eradication and destruction tear apart the historical remnants that generation after generation of the Muslims prided themselves with the immense honour of serving and preserving.

The strangest thing in all this is that the Shaykhs of Najd see very well the extent to which the Islamic World disapproves of this and its profound anger at this innovation that looks down upon the early Consensus of the Muslims and makes light of the symbols of their faith. They see this, yet they do not turn to address the Muslims with one word by which they might try to justify their actions and explain their viewpoint. For the way it ought to be – if we suppose the Shaykhs of Najd were right in those acts of theirs while the Ulema of the Islamic World in their entirety are ignorant and wrong – is that those Shaykhs address the Muslim World with a clear demonstration of what they personally know, so that the Muslim World should realise its [supposed] mistake and redirect itself to the right way. For the Muslim World always distinguished itself and stood out from the rest of the world in knowing the right. By so doing, they [the Shaykhs of Najd] would earn the reward of guiding and directing the Muslims to the truth from which they had [presumably] erred through all their past ages.

On this occasion I shall relate the following story which began but, until now, remains open-ended.

We complained to one another, I and my most esteemed friend, [the Saudi Minister of Religious Endowments] al-Ustadh Dr. 'Abd Allah ibn 'Abd al-Muhsin al-Turki, when we met during a conference held in one of our Arabic countries, about this **grievous state which has practically given birth to a new Islam from the land of Najd without any connection to the pious Predecessors at all! Subsequent to which, this**

situation has now caused the worst manifestations of mutual destruction and division in the Islamic world, and even in most Islamic centres in Europe and America.

Dr. 'Abd Allah said to me: "This is truly a sad state of affairs. But what is the solution?"

I said: "The solution is for us to try to speak to those brothers and discuss together all the issues according to the criteria of Islamic knowledge. If there is real sincerity without mistrust nor ill will in our endeavours, then surely, knowledge will lead us to the truth and truth to success!"

We agreed, on this basis, to organise a scholarly congress in the Saudi Kingdom formed of ten of the Saudi scholars who possess ample knowledge, sincerity in the Religion of Allah, and jealous concern over the unity of the Community of Islam, together with ten scholars from the rest of the Arab World possessing the same qualities.[10] Their task would be to examine among themselves those newly invented questions which have no precedent among the pious Predecessors as far as we know. They would discuss them according to a mutually agreed-upon scholarly method. It was hoped that, at that time, the real answers would manifest themselves and dissipate the clouds and illusions that caused misperceptions which led into factionalism and the paths of misguidance.

We parted on that note. I promised to provide a list of ten scholars from various quarters of our Arab world, at its forefront Syria, just as he also promised to provide the names of ten scholars from the [Saudi] Kingdom, after which a venue would be set and the meeting should take place.

---

[10] One wonders why the non-Arab remainder of the Islamic world – four fifths of the *Umma* – were not included for representation in this agreement, especially Turkish ulema (Turkey being arguably the second largest holder of Prophetic and Companion relics in the world), Indian ulema, African and South-East Asian ulema, etc. [T]

I fulfilled my promise and sent him the names of the ten scholars in which I saw the qualities of ample knowledge, sincerity in the Religion of Allah, and jealous concern over the unity of the Muslims. I then waited, expecting to receive from him the remainder of the names and the time and place of the congress. And here I am, still waiting, years after this initial agreement!!

I came to know that my loyal friend had done his best and left no stone unturned in order to choose, among the scholars of the [Saudi] Kingdom, those deemed most qualified to take part in such a congress. However, as is their habit, they run from confrontation and discussion of these very issues to the same extent that they rush eagerly, as individuals, to implement their opinions – which they alone hold – concerning the same issues!!

Accordingly, we need to ask ourselves and each other the question: Is this the way of sincerity for the sake of Allah in establishing the good and eliminating evil?

How can the good be good if we – brothers in Islam – do not call upon one another in complete cooperation as to recognize the good and make it known to others? And how can evil be [known as] evil in our Islamic practice if we do not call upon one another in complete cooperation so as to recognize it as evil, following which, help each other to denounce it as such?

How can our brothers the Shaykhs of Najd single themselves out in committing these strange acts which Sayyid Yusuf al-Rifaʿi has listed in this engaging epistle and which amount to fifty-[seven][11] strange acts? After much researching, we have not found, in the Religion of Allah, the least

[11] The original text states "fifty-eight." Sayyid Yusuf actually mentions more items than the fifty-seven he numbers as some of his entries cite multiple offences. Cf. §3, 9, 11, 12, 25, 26, 43, 49, 52. [T]

justification for their committing them. I say: **How can the fact that the Shaykhs of Najd single themselves out from the totality of the ulema of the Muslims in committing those newly invented acts of theirs, without any previous consultation or cooperation with them, be an Islamically acceptable deed when al-Islam was and does not cease to be, in all its important affairs, firmly established on mutual communication and cooperation?** Yet I do not despair. I remain full of hope as long as I find a way to retain hope.

I thank my brother, al-Sayyid Yusuf al-Rifaʿi, for his dialogue in the form of an epistle, its important content, and its endearing and gentle style. At the same time, I hope that this work will find receptive ears among the eminent brethren to whom it is directed. Likewise, I hope that we shall begin to notice, on their part, the heartfelt fervor of sincerity for the sake of Allah, jealous concern over what Allah has made sacred, and tender pity in keeping family ties in the fold of the kinship of Islam.

I also hope that this epistle will remind them that Islam does not become complete in a human being until it enters the mind as complete certitude and holds sway over the heart as love and utter veneration.

Will you now check and see, O scholars of Najd! the place of love for Allah and His Prophet in your hearts? Will you try and cultivate such love – in case you find it atrophied in yourselves – through more remembrance of Allah? When you do, then such love will certainly motivate you – I swear it by Allah! – to protect and guard the historical remnants of Prophethood and their owner instead of eradicating and destroying them. You will then walk the path of the pious Predecessors in this respect. You will, once and for all, cease uttering that word which you think is advice but which is, in fact, a perverse lie, and which you think is an easy matter but which is, in the sight of Allah, a grave and tremendous matter! I

mean your statement to the pilgrims on many occasions: "Beware of exaggeration in love for the Messenger of Allah!"

If you had only said, as the Messenger of Allah ﷺ said: "Do not over-extol me the way the Christians over-extolled the son of Maryam," it would have been acceptable discourse and valuable advice. As for love that consists in the attachment of the heart to the beloved in the sense that one feels ease and familiarity near him and estrangement far from him: to exaggerate in such love – when the beloved is the Messenger of Allah ﷺ – is nothing but a patent sign of added nearness to Allah when we know full well that love in Allah is among the necessary constituents of [declaring and upholding] the Oneness of Allah.

And, as much as the lover of the Messenger of Allah ﷺ exaggerates in his love for him or overdoes it, still, he will never reach more than the extent ordered by the Messenger of Allah ﷺ who said, as narrated by the two Grandmasters [al-Bukhari and Muslim]: "None of you [truly] believes until I am more beloved to him than his property and children and all people" and, in another narration in al-Bukhari: "and himself."

When your hearts bloom with this kind of love, you will realise that, as much as they become imbued with such love, they shall still fall short of the level which the Messenger of Allah ﷺ deserves. Your souls will thirst to see the historical remnants of Prophethood – if any such remnants still remain with you today – instead of detesting them and frantically using every means to rid yourselves of them and eliminate them!

I ask Allah and beg Him to reunite us on Truth with our brothers the scholars of Najd, the Truth brought by the Book of Allah and shown by the life of the Messenger of Allah ﷺ and his Sunna, according to which our pious Predecessors lived. May He reunite us – after [granting us] certitude of mind in the realities of Islam – on an unsuppressed regular devotion (*wird*) consisting in love of Allah and love of His Prophet ﷺ.

- *Dr. Muhammad Said Ramadan al-Buti.*

ADVICE

TO OUR BROTHERS
THE SCHOLARS OF

NAJD

(1420/1999)

Sayyid

Yusuf Hashim al-Rifa'i

In the Name of Allah All-Beneficent Most Merciful

Say: Who gives you provision from the sky and the earth? Say: Allah. Lo! we or you assuredly are rightly guided or in error manifest. Say: You will not be asked of what we committed, nor shall we be asked of what you do. Say: Our Lord will bring us all together, then He will judge between us with truth. He is the All-Knowing Judge (34:24-26).

Lo! Allah enjoins justice and kindness, and giving to kinsfolk, and forbids lewdness and abomination and wickedness. He exhorts you in order that you may take heed (16:90).

O my people! Yours is the kingdom today, you being uppermost in the land. But who would save us from the wrath of Allah should it reach us? (40:20).

All praise belongs to Allah! Blessings and greetings upon our Master [Muhammad] the Messenger of Allah and upon his Family and most honourable Companions and all those loyal to him.

To proceed: Using as my point of departure the narration of the Prophet ﷺ: "Religion is sincere, faithful advice. We said: [Faithful] to whom? He replied: To Allah; to His Book; and to His Messenger, the leaders of the Muslims, and their multitude,"[12] and after the publication of my book *al-Radd al-Muhkam al-Mani'* and that of other books authored by people of learning,[13] I waited to see if, perhaps, some of your doings and methods would change. However, nothing of the sort took place.

Therefore, since Allah says in Surat al-'Asr: **By the declining day, Lo! man is in a state of loss, Save those who believe and do good works, and exhort one another to truth and exhort one another to endurance** (103:1-3), I decided, after the Prayer of Counsel *(al-istikhâra)*, to address you with this sincere faithful advice which, I hope, will be accepted. I ask our Lord Most High to show us and you the truth for what it is and grant us to follow it, and show us falsehood for what it is and grant us to avoid it. May He not make this matter confused for us lest we follow our lusts. It is Allah alone Who guides to what is right.

Accordingly, I say, trusting in Allah for success:

---

[12] See below, #39. [T]

[13] Cf. 'Abd al-Hayy al-'Amrawi & 'Abd al-Karim Murad, *al-Tahdhir min alIghtirar bi ma Ja'a fi Kitab al-Hiwar min al-Manakir* ("Warning Against Being Fooled by the Reprehensible Contents of the Book [by Ibn Mani'] 'A Debate with al-Maliki'"); Shaykh Rashid ibn Ibrahim al-Marikhi of Bahrayn, *Raf' al-Astar 'an Shubuhat wa Dalalat Sahib al-Hiwar* ("Exposing the Insinuations and Aberrations of the Author of the 'Debate with al-Maliki'"); al-Sayyid 'Abd Allah ibn Mahfuz al-Haddad Ba 'Alawi al-Hadrami, *al-Sunna wa al-Bid'a*. Etc. [T]

1. Calling the Muslims: "Pagans"

It is not permitted to charge Muslims – believers in monotheism who pray with you, fast, pay *zakât*, and perform pilgrimage shouting over and over, "Ever at Your call, O Allah! Ever at Your call, there is no partner with You, ever at Your call! Truly all glory and praise, all favour and grace belong to You, and all sovereignty and dominion! No-one can be a partner to You!" – It is not permitted, by Law, to charge them with idolatry (*al-shirk*) the way your books and publications are filled with such charges; the way your preacher clamours on the day of the Major Hajj in the mosque of al-Khayf in Mina, the eve of the Feast of the pilgrims and all Muslims; and the way his fellow preacher frightens the people of Makka and those in the Holy Mosque on the Day of 'Id al-Fitr through all their verbal assaults and false accusations. Stop this, and may Allah guide you! To frighten a Muslim is prohibited, especially the dwellers of the Two Sanctuaries. There are many sound sacred texts to that effect.

2. Calling the Muslims: "Apostates"

You have declared the Sufis disbelievers then the Ash'aris. You have denied and denounced imitation of and adherence to the Four Imams (Abu Hanifa, Malik, al-Shafi'i, Ahmad ibn Hanbal) whereas their imitators formed and continue to form the vastest mass (*al-sawâd al-a'zam*) of the Muslims, just as the official ideology of your state and that instituted by King 'Abd al-'Aziz – may Allah have mercy on him! – textually stipulates reliance upon, and due consideration of the Four *Madhâhib*. Therefore, stop this, and may Allah guide you! Whoever turns disbeliever after his Islam has the status of an apostate (*murtadd*) whose killing becomes licit. Therefore, remember the narration of your Prophet the Elect One – Allah bless and greet him and his Family: "Do not revert after me and turn disbelievers again, striking at one another's neck."[14]

3. Calling the Muslims: "Deviants"

After you finished doing the above, you let loose certain hirelings you had nurtured, so that they began to throw accusations of misguidance and deviance at the Islamic groups and organisations that work in the field of calling to Islam (da'wa) and are active raising up the Word of Allah and commanding good and forbidding evil. I mean organisations such as Jama'at al-Tabligh; al-Ikhwan al-Muslimin; the Deobandi group that represents the brightest Ulema of India, Pakistan, and Bangladesh; and the Barelwi group that represents the vastest mass of the common Muslims in those countries. In so doing they have made use of books, tapes, and the like. Then you went and translated those books into various languages, distributing them free through your numerous outlets. Likewise, you published a book that contains the declaration that the people of Abu Dhabi and Dubai are disbelievers, together with the Ibadis,[15] your colleagues on the board of Majlis al-Ta'awun. As for your attacks on the renowned Azhar University and its scholars, they are too numerous to count!

[14] Narrated from Ibn 'Umar and Jarir (may Allah be well pleased with them) by al-Bukhari and Muslim

[15] The Ibadiyya are a Khariji madhhab founded by 'Abd Allah ibn Ibad al-Tamimi (d. 86) who consider the Muslims who differ with them to be neither mu'mins nor mushriks but kuffār ni'ma i.e. thankless sinners but not apostates, whose lives are sacred and their regions within Dār al-Islam, and they allow intermarriage with and inheritance from and to them. Cf. Abu Zahra, Tarikh al-Madhahib al-Islamiyya (1:85, 2:54). [T]

4. Calling the Muslims: "Innovators"

You keep repeating the phrase of the noble hadith, "Every innovation is misguidance"[16] without discernment, only to criticise and condemn others, yet approving certain actions that contradict the Prophetic Sunna without condemning them nor counting them as innovations. We shall list some of them.

5. Shutting the Mosque in Madina at Night

You shut close the Mosque of the Messenger of Allah ﷺ after the 'Isha prayer when this Mosque was never closed before your time in the history of the Muslims, preventing people from performing retreat (*i'tikâf*) and late night prayers (*tahajjud*) in it, and you forget the saying of Allah Most High: **And who does greater wrong than he who forbids the approach to the sanctuaries of Allah lest His Name should be mentioned therein, and strives for their ruin?...** (2:114).

6. Imposing the Style of Najd in Adhân

You impose on the callers to prayer in the Hijaz a specific style of *adhân* which is the one you use in Najd, within a specific, limited duration of time, and you require that the voice not be softened nor beautified in calling the Muslims to this paramount symbol of the Religion which is *Salât*.

7. Monopolising Teaching in Hijaz

You forbid teaching and admonition in the Two Sanctuaries even if the teacher is one of the great Muslim scholars and even if he comes from the

[16] Narrated from Jabir ibn 'Abd Allah (may Allah be well-pleased with him) by Muslim. See Sayyid 'Abd Allah ibn al-Siddiq al-Ghumari's *Itqan al-Sun'a fi Tahqiq Ma'na al-Bid'a*

Hijaz or al-Ahsa' as long as he does not follow your school of thought or carry an explicit permit written and sealed by you. Anyone other than yourselves is thus barred, were it the Rector of the distinguished al-Azhar! Therefore, fear Allah and do not go to excess in promoting your *madhhab* but keep a good opinion of your brothers among the scholars of Islam.

8. Preventing Burial in al-Baqiʿ

You forbid the burial of Muslims who die outside Madina and Makka from taking place in those Two Cities which are of the most blessed sites loved by Allah and His Prophet ﷺ, depriving the Muslims from obtaining the immense reward of burial in them. It is related from ʿAbd Allah ibn ʿAdi al-Zuhri (may Allah be well-pleased with him) that he said: "I saw the Prophet ﷺ on his mount, standing on the hillock, saying: 'By Allah! You are surely the best land of Allah and the most beloved to Allah of the lands of Allah, and if I were not being driven out of you I would never go out.'"[17]

It is also narrated from Ibn ʿUmar (may Allah be well-pleased with him) that he said the Messenger of Allah ﷺ said: "Whoever can die in al-Madina, let him die in it, for I do intercede for whoever dies in it."[18]

9. Obstructing and Scolding Women in Madina

You forbid women from reaching the Place of the Noble Meeting (*al-Muwâjaha al-Sharîfa*) at the grave of the Prophet ﷺ and greeting him just as men do. If you could, you would prevent women from circumambulating the Holy House with their lawful relatives, all contrary to

[17] Narrated by Ahmad, al-Tirmidhi (*hasan gharîb sahîh*), al-Nasa'i in *al-Sunan al-Kubra* (2:479), Ibn Majah, Ibn Hibban (9:22 #3708), and al-Hakim (3:7 *sahîh al-isnâd*).
[18] Narrated by Ahmad, al-Nasa'i in *al-Kubra* (2:488), al-Tirmidhi from Ayyub al-Sikhtyani (*hasan gharîb*), Ibn Majah, and Ibn Hibban (9:57 #3741).

the practice of the pious Predecessors and the Muslims! You despise the believing women who protect their honour and worship their Lord. You rebuke them harshly, block them from seeing the [original] Mosque and the imam with multiple barriers, and stare at them with suspicion and distrust. All this is an ugly innovation for it is the start of something that did not take place in the time of the Prophet ﷺ nor that of the pious Predecessors. For the rows of the men used to stand behind the imam, then those of the boys, then those of the women, all praying together without barrier behind the Prophet ﷺ.

10. Posting Hoodlums at the Noble Grave

You have brought hirelings and ignoramuses whose only skill is frowning and placed them at the Muwâjaha Sharîfa with their backs turned to the Elect Prophet ﷺ. They turn their backs and rear ends to him, facing his visitors and all Muslims with sour faces full of spite, giving them sinister looks and taunting them with charges of idolatry and innovation, almost attacking them physically. They rebuke this one, bark at that one, hit the [supplicating] hands of the third, raising their voices to censor and blame, ignoring and forgetting the saying of Allah: **O you who believe! Lift not up your voices above the voice of the Prophet, nor shout when speaking to him as you shout one to another, lest your works be rendered vain while you perceive not. Lo! they who subdue their voices in the presence of the Messenger of Allah, those are they whose hearts Allah has proven unto righteousness. Theirs will be forgiveness and immense reward. Lo! those who call you from behind the private apartment, most of them have no sense (49:2-4).**

All this behaviour is compounded with arrogance and is compounded with arrogance and persistence in humiliating the lovers and beloved of al-Mustafa ﷺ and his visitors among the Believers in his noble presence and right before his noble sleeping-ground[19] which the Shaykh of the Hanbalis [Abu al-Wafaʼ] Ibn ʻAqil considered the most sublime spot in all the universe as related by Shaykh Ibn al-Qayyim in his book *Badaʼiʻ al-Fawaʼid*.

11. Blocking Women from Visiting Baqiʻ

You forbid women from visiting the noble Baqiʻ with no agreed-upon, clear and explicit proof from the Law. You create difficulties for the Muslims who perform visitation in other than short and restricted times. Some of them wait for the opportunity of burying the dead so that they can visit al-Baqiʻ! You have also forbidden guides to al-Madina al-Munawwara from accompanying visitors, eliminating their livelihoods and leaving visitors in confusion. They do not know the location of the graves of the noble Family of the Prophet ﷺ nor those of his wives the Mothers of the Believers, nor those of his Companions (may Allah be well-pleased with them) and this is truly grave injustice, tyranny, oppression, and arrogance which Allah shall never accept nor His most honourable Prophet ﷺ. Stop it, and may Allah Most High guide you!

12. Grave Destruction and Desecration

You destroyed the sign-posts by which we knew the graves of the Companions, the Mothers of the Believers, and the members of the noble Family of Prophet ﷺ. You left them a vacant lot, the grave-posts scattered

---

[19] See Ibn al-Qayyim, *Badaʼiʻ* (3:135-136=2:147) where he states that Ibn ʻAqil said: "Someone asked me which was better, the room of the Prophet ﷺ or the Kaʻba? I replied, If you merely mean the room, then the Kaʻba is better. But if you mean the room with him in it then no, by Allah! nor the Throne and its bearers, nor the Paradise of ʻAdn, nor the revolving universes! For in that room there is a body which, if it were weighed against this world and the next, would outweigh it." And Imam Malik said: "The spot which contains the body of the Prophet ﷺ is better than anything else, even the Seat of Authority (*al-Kursi*) and the Throne (*al-ʻArsh*); then the Mosque of the Prophet ﷺ; then Makka."

stones so that we no longer know whose grave is where. Gasoline was even poured on one of them.[20] Truly there is no change nor power except with Allah Most High, Most Great. Leave stone superstructures intact for they are allowed! Leave the handspan elevation for it is allowed, together with the two grave-posts! It is established that the Prophet ﷺ placed a rock on top of 'Uthman ibn Maz'un's (may Allah be well-pleased with him) grave saying: "With it I shall designate the grave of my [milk-]brother and later bury in it whoever dies among my relatives."[21] Kharija ibn Zayd said: "I can see myself when we were young men in the time of 'Uthman [ibn 'Affan] (may Allah be well-pleased with him). The strongest one of us in high jump was he who could jump over the grave of 'Uthman ibn Maz'un and clear it."[22]

13. Police Interrogation Centres

You created an inquest and trial centre in the corner of the Prophetic Sanctuary previously, now next to al-Baqi'. There, you sentence those you observe to use intermediaries (*tawassul*), or visit frequently, or act humbly, weep or supplicate Allah in front of the most noble grave, seeking the Prophet ﷺ as a means of approach to Allah. **You shower them with a hail of questions prepared in advance pertaining to the licitness of Visitation, using intermediaries, and [celebrating] the noble Birth.**

---

[20] The grave of Amina bint Wahb the Prophet's ﷺ mother.

[21] Narrated from an unnamed Companion by Abu Dawud and al-Bayhaqi in *al-Kubra* (3:412) with fair chains cf. Ibn Hajar, *Talkhis al-Habir* (2:134); Ibn al-Mulaqqin, *Tuhfat al-Muhtaj* (2:29). The complete report states that the Prophet ﷺ asked a man to place a rock on top of Ibn Maz'un's grave; when he was unable to move it, he ﷺ rolled up his sleeves and helped him and the whiteness of his arms was visible. Ibn Maz'un was the first of the *Muhājirūn* buried in Baqi' al-Gharqad. Ibrahim, the Prophet's ﷺ son, was buried next to him. [T]

[22] Cited by al-Bukhari without chain in his *Sahih* chapter-title, "[Placing] a Stalk on Top of the Grave." Ibn Hajar said in *Fath al-Bari* (3:256=1959 ed. 3:223): "Al-Bukhari narrated it with its [sound] chain in *al-Tarikh al-Saghir* (1:42)... It contains a proof for the licitness of raising high the grave and elevating it above the surface of the earth."

Whoever you deem in violation in the above you imprison, cancel his residency permit, and banish from the land. All this when these are, in fact, matters that turn between the status of desirability (*istihbâb*) and that of indifference (*ibâha*) among the scholars, including the Hanbalis, so that it is impermissible to declare apostate a Muslim on their basis or pursue him in justice. I was told by a trustworthy former detainee that his hands remained chained all the while of his month-long incarceration so that he performed ablution and prayed in chains. He was even prevented from reading the Holy Qur'an. Fear Allah! Injustice shall reap multi-layered darkness on the Day of Resurrection! Can such evil take place in the Mosque of the Prophet ﷺ who said: "I am only a mercy offered"?[23] Allah sent him as a mercy to all the worlds: what about the Muslims you treat so harshly in close vicinity to him in his own Mosque? Remember he said, "Prophets are alive in their grave, praying"; "Truly Allah forbade the earth to consume the bodies of Prophets."[24]

14.   Razing of the Mosque of Abu Bakr

(may Allah be well-pleased with him)

You allowed a generous donor from Madina to raze and rebuild the mosque of Abu Bakr al-Siddiq (may Allah be well-pleased with him) in Jabal al-Khandaq at his expense.[25] Once the building was razed, you cancelled the rebuilding permit for you consider it an innovation to visit the seven

---

[23] Narrated from Abu Hurayra by al-Bayhaqi in his *Shu'ab* (2:164) and Dala'il (1:157); al-Quda'i in his *Musnad* (2:189); al-Hakim (1:35=1:91 *sahîh*, al-Dhahabi concurred. Al-Bazzar (3:114) and al-Tabarani in *al-Saghir* and *al-Awsat* (1:168) narrate it as: "I was sent only as a mercy offered" with *Sahih* narrators as per al-Haythami (8:257).

[24] See al-Maliki's *The Life of the Prophets in Their Graves* for documentation of these sound narrations [T].

[25] On their destruction of Albanian Kosovar religious monuments, graveyards, and Ottoman-style mosques, see Stephen Suleiman Schwartz, "Letter from the Balkans" in The Muslim Magazine vol. 3 (1-2 Winter/Spring 2000) p. 25-26, section titled, "Reaction to Wahhabi Reconstruction." [T]

Mosques at the site of the Battle of the Trench, concerning which was revealed Surat al-Ahzab! In fact, you wish to destroy them all.

15.   Interdiction of "Dala'il al-Khayrat"

You forbid people to bring in and read *Dala'il al-Khayrat fi alSalawat ʿala al-Nabi* ("Guide to All Good Things in the Invocation of Blessings upon the Prophet ﷺ") by the knower of Allah and descendant of al-Hasan (may Allah be well-pleased with him), Shaykh Muhammad Sulayman al-Jazuli and other books. Yet you know of the books and magazines that enter the land and are put on display, all sorts of publications deemed abominable and reprehensible by the Law. Fear Allah!

16.   Forbidding Mawlid Gatherings

You spy on, harass, arrest, and punish whoever holds gatherings of celebration and commemoration of the Prophetic birth are devoid of any lawfully reprehensible activity. Yet you do not object to gatherings of entertainment, musical instruments, singing, and all such displays. Since when is it allowed to use a double standard, humiliating the loving faithful while cajoling the mindless dissolute?

17.   Forbidding Qunût in the Fajr Prayer

You forbid the imams in the mosques to recite the *qunût* supplication in the dawn prayer, deeming it an innovation when you know that it is established in the Law according to two of the four Imams – al-Shafiʿi and Malik. Why do you impose your own opinion and create difficulties for the Muslims?

18. Monopolising the Position of Imam

You do not allow anyone to be imam in either of the Two Sanctuaries except one of your own. You make it categorically forbidden to the Ulema of al-Hijaz, al-Ahsa', and others. Is this an act of justice, or an obligation of the Religion? Fear Allah and be just! For Allah loves those who are just.

19. Destruction of Our Historical Vestiges

You have wreaked destruction on the historical vestiges of the Prophet ﷺ and those of his most honourable Companions (may Allah be well-pleased with them) in Madina al-Munawwara especially and the two Sanctuaries generally. Nothing seems to remain of these vestiges anymore except the Prophetic Mosque itself. Yet, in our time, the nations of the world pride themselves in and preserve their historical vestiges as a memento, a lesson, a meaningful sign of their time-honoured past. But you consider that every vestige that is stopped at for perusal or visit, is a partner [worshipped] together with Allah. But Allah Himself ordered us to travel the earth to see the vestiges of the idolaters and derive lessons from them, such as 'Ad and Thamud, found at Diyar Salih, al-'Ala', near Madina al-Munawwara, which are still visited sites, as Allah said: **Systems have passed away before you. Do but travel in the land and see the nature of the consequence for those who did deny (the messengers)** (3:137). **Have they not travelled in the land to see the nature of the consequence for those who disbelieved before them? They were mightier than these in power and (in the) traces (which they left behind them) in the earth. Yet Allah seized them for their sins, and they had no protector from Allah. That was because their messengers kept bringing them clear proofs (of Divine sovereignty) but they disbelieved; so Allah seized them. Lo! He is Strong, Severe in punishment** (40:21-22). **Has not the history of those before you reached you: the folk of Noah and (the tribes of) 'Ad**

and Thamud and those after them? None but Allah knows them.
Their messengers came unto them with clear proofs, but they thrust
their hands into their mouths, and said: Lo! we disbelieve in that
wherewith you have been sent, and lo! we are in grave doubt
concerning that to which you call us (14:9). Why then do you deprive the
Muslims from witnessing the sign-posts and vestiges of the battles of Badr,
Uhud, Hudaybiya, Hunayn, al-Ahzab, and others of the Days of Allah in
which He gave victory to His Messenger and righteous servants, routing
idolatry and the polytheists? Fear Allah, and be among those endowed with
hearts so that, perhaps, you will be granted mercy!

20.   Aiding the Arch-Innovator, al-Albani

You have provided a haven to Nasir Albani[26] and abetted him,
allowing him to publish his book *Ahkam al-Jana'iz wa Bida'uha* in which
he openly asks for the removal of the grave of the Prophet ﷺ from the
most noble Mosque![27] You appointed him a member in the upper board of
the Islamic University in Madina al-Munawwara and a teacher in it. After
the late King Faysal barred him and expelled him from the country with
some of his followers you returned him to that position. You still liberally
propagate and recommend his deviant books but have interdicted and
forbidden some of the books of Hujjat al-Islam al-Ghazzali, Abu al-Hasan
al-Nadwi, 'Abd al-Fattah Abu Ghudda, al-Maliki, Sa'id Hawwa, al-Buti, and
others of the Ulema of the Muslims. Where is justice and equity?

21.   Aiding Another Rabid Extremist

You nurtured al-Albani's student and deputy in Kuwait, 'Abd
al-Rahman 'Abd al-Khaliq, directing your followers to him, lavishly

---

[26] When he was banned from Syria before his expulsion from Saudi Arabia. He lived
under house arrest in Amman until his death in 1999. [T]
[27] He reiterates this foolishness in his *Tahdhir al-Sajid*, *Hijjat al-Nabi*, and *Manasik
al-Hajj wa al-'Umra*. [T]

supporting him with every means. He assailed the host of the Friends of Allah in his *Fada'ih al-Sufiyya* ("The Disgraces of the Sufis") in which he deems all Sufis misguided, free-thinking heretics (*zanâdiqa*) and lawless esotericists (*bâtiniyyîn*) even if they count those eulogised by Ibn Taymiyya, Ibn Rajab, al-Dhahabi, and the rest of your putative authorities! Remember a rigorously authentic *hadith qudsî* states: "Whoever shows enmity to a single friend of Mine, I declare war on him."[28]

22.   Erasing Poetry in Praise of the Prophet

صلى الله
عليه وسلم

You take advantage, every year, of the opportunity of maintaining, polishing, and refurbishing the Prophetic Mosque in order to eliminate many of the emblems of Islam [still] found in the inner hall of the Mosque such as historical vestiges and praises of the Prophet ﷺ. Thus you painted over many of the verses of al-Busayri's poem on the Prophetic Mantle (*al-Burda*).[29] You have also tried to cover up the famous two verses – inscribed on the windows of the Mosque – quoted in the story of al-'Utbi as mentioned by Ibn Kathir in his Tafsir: "*O best of those whose bones are buried in the deep earth, and from whose fragrance the depth and height have become sweet! / May I be the ransom for a grave in which you dwell, where one finds purity, bounty and munificence!*[30] If the Custodian of the Two Sanctuaries – King Fahd – had not stopped you when the news reached him then ordered you to restore them as they were...! But what is the reason for this disrespect and obstruction of your most noble Prophet ﷺ, the means of access between you and your Lord? What has transpired between you and him? You seem to have forgotten His saying: **Those who vex the messenger of Allah, for them there is a painful doom** (9:61) and **Lo! those who**

---

[28] Part of a hadith narrated from Abu Hurayra by Bukhari.
[29] See its explanations in Shaykh H. Kabbani's *Encyclopedia of Islamic Doctrine* (2:83-141). [T]
[30] Ibn Kathir, *Tafsir* (2:306) and *al-Bidaya* (1:180). [T]

malign Allah and His messenger, Allah has cursed them in the world and the Hereafter, and has prepared for them the doom of the disdained (33:57).

23.   Asking to Demolish the Green Dome

You allowed a man by the name of Muqbil ibn Hadi al-Wadi'i – known through his books and tapes for his propensity to insult and disparage those of the Ulema who disagree with him, those who call unto Allah, and the pious of this Community of Islam – to produce some research at the end of his studies at the Islamic University of Madina titled "About the Dome Built over the Grave of the Messenger ﷺ" sponsored by Shaykh Hammad al-Ansari. In this paper he demands openly and without shame that the Noble Grave be brought out of the Mosque, deems the presence of the Grave and Noble Dome there major innovations, and asks that they both be destroyed! On top of this you granted him high marks and a passing grade!

Do you honour those who challenge the Messenger of Islam, the Beloved of Allah, the Mercy to the Universes and His Intimate Friend?! Then this man directed hundreds of his followers, imitators, and their kind among those influenced by your School, bearing arms, to destroy and unearth the graves of the pious Muslims in Aden, Yemen, a few years ago.[31] They roamed the land spreading corruption and ruin, digging up the graves of the dead with picks and spades until they brought out the bones of some of the dead and violated their sanctity. They caused a deaf and blind dissension. We heard they even used dynamite in some places! **All this is part of the record of your deeds.**

---

[31] First among them Imam al-Habib al-'Aydarus al-'Adani [Abu Bakr ibn 'Abd Allah (d. 911)] the blessing of Aden and Hadramawt, Allah have mercy on him! Allah thwarted their plans and his shrine was renewed and blessed dome rebuilt.

24.   Not Saying "al-Munawwara" for Madina

You named the volume of the Qur'an printed on order of the
Custodian of the Two Sanctuaries – Allah reward him for it! – by the name
of *Mushaf al-Madina al-Nabawiyya* ("Volume of the Prophetic City")
instead of *Mushaf al-Madina al-Munawwara* ("Volume of the Illuminated
City"). It seems you refuse to acknowledge that this blessed city became
illuminated – as did the entire world – by the sending and messengership of
our Master Muhammad ﷺ. Yet the young girls of the Ansar called out in
the past: "The full moon rose over us from the mountains of al-Wada'!" For
the Prophet ﷺ is indeed *al-Badr* – the full moon – and the Light, as
Allah said: **O Prophet! Lo! We have sent you as a witness and a bringer
of good tidings and a warner, and as a summoner unto Allah by His
permission, and as a lamp that gives light** (33:45-46), **and Now has
come unto you light from Allah and a plain Scripture whereby Allah
guides him who seeks His good pleasure unto paths of peace. He
brings them out of darkness unto light by His decree, and guides
them unto a straight path** (5:15-16). Go back to the books of
commentary and you will see that they explained the light mentioned in the
foregoing verses to mean al-Mustafa ﷺ. Here we will not argue with you
concerning the light of his noble essence but we say that he was Light and
Mercy through the Book and the Sunna and guidance that he brought. Allah
said: **He brings them out of darkness unto light by His decree and
guides them unto a straight path** (5:16).

25.   Not Saying "Sanctuary" for Madina

You insist on naming the overseeing board for the affairs of the Two
Sanctuaries, "Presidency of the Meccan Sanctuary and the Noble Prophetic
Mosque" (*ri'âsat al-haram al-makkî wa al-masjid al-nabawî al-sharîf*) but
you do not say, "the Noble Prophetic Sanctuary" (*al-haram al-nabawî*

al-*sharîf*). Likewise in your road signs indicating that direction. Why is not his Mosque [referred to as] a Sanctuary?

The Prophet ﷺ declared all of Madina a sanctuary. 'Asim ibn Sulayman al-Ahwal said that he asked Anas: "Did the Messenger of Allah ﷺ make Madina a sanctuary (*haram*)?" He said: "Yes! from such-and-such a place to such-and-such a place. So, whoever gives rise to some innovation in it" – Anas said to 'Asim, "and this is a very tough stipulation" – "incurs the curse of Allah, the angels, and all people! Nor will Allah accept from him the least barter and trade on the Day of Resurrection!"

Another narration – also from Anas – states: "Then he ﷺ marched until Uhud came into sight and said: 'This is a mountain who loves us and whom we love.' Then, overlooking al-Madina, he said: 'O Allah! Truly I am declaring a sanctuary all that is between its two mountains as Ibrahim declared Makka a sanctuary. O Allah! grant them blessings in their *mudd* and *sâ*' [measures].'"[32]

Also narrated from Abu Hurayra, the Prophet ﷺ said: "Al-Madina is a sanctuary (*al-madînatu haram*), so whoever gives rise to an innovation in it or gives safe haven to an innovator, let the curse of Allah be on him, that of the angels, and that of All people! And let not the least barter nor trade be accepted from him on the Day of Resurrection!"[33]

26.   Falsifying Our Scholarly Heritage

It has become your custom to suppress whatever does not please or satisfy you from the books of our Islamic heritage which you cannot prevent from entering the [Saudi] Kingdom because the general public need them.

[32] Narrated by al-Bukhari and Muslim.
[33] Narrated by Muslim.

This is a criminal act both in Islamic Law and in secular laws against the views of the authors who are Ulema of the pious Predecessors. They cannot summon you before a judge in this world but they can certainly summon you before the Almighty Judge in the next... Among the passages that were suppressed or altered and tampered with:

1. In the book of *al-Adhkar* by Imam Muhyi al-Din al-Nawawi as published by Dar al-Huda in al-Riyad in 1409/1989 and edited by 'Abd al-Qadir al-Arna'ut of Damascus, page 295, the chapter-title, "Section on Visiting the Grave of the Messenger ﷺ" was substituted with the title, "Section on Visiting the Mosque of the Messenger of Allah ﷺ" together with the suppression of several lines from the beginning of the section and its end, and the suppression of al-'Utbi's story which Imam al-Nawawi had mentioned in full. This is a bold felony against an author and his book! When the editor was asked about it, he replied that your agents were the ones who had changed and tampered. I have a facsimile of his own hand-written statement to that effect.

2. Certain expressions that displeased you were suppressed from al-Sawi's [d. 1241/1825] supercommentary on *Tafsir al-Jalalayn*.[34]

3. Suppression of the chapter that concerns the Friends of Allah (*alawliyâ'*), Substitute-Saints (*al-abdâl*), and the Righteous (*al-sâlihîn*) from Ibn 'Abidin's Hashiya in Hanafi jurisprudence.[35]

4. Suppression of the 10th volume – on *tasawwuf* – of Ibn Taymiyya's *Fatawa* in your latest edition.

[34] *Hashiya 'ala Tafsir al-Jalalay*n (v. 58:18-19), passage describing modern Kharijism from which were removed the words, "namely, a sect in the Hijaz named Wahhabis" [T].

[35] More probably *Ijabat al-Ghawth bi Bayan Hal al-Abdal wa al-Ghawth* in Ibn 'Abidin's *Rasa'il* (2:264-284). [T]

5.	Shaykh Ibn Baz the [late] former overall president of the directorships of scholarly research, *iftâ'*, *da'wa*, and *irshâd* tried to rectify whatever did not please him in *Fath al-Bari* by the Imam and hadith master Ibn Hajar al-'Asqalani. So he published three volumes together with his aides then stopped his remarks; but he opened an avenue of harm and evil with these remarks.

6.	Abu Bakr al-Jaza'iri was given the opportunity to make a commentary on the Qur'an that might be a substitute and rival to *Tafsir al-Jalalayn*. The public was then misled to believe that they were the same book to ensure its propagation.

## 27.	Indecencies of Guards towards Women

Whereas you separate women from their relatives in the Mosque of the Prophet ﷺ on the pretence that you are anxious to preserve chastity and Religion, you station your men at the entrances reserved to women, fully facing them, as if those men were divinely immunised against all that may occur in others. Likewise you station your male observers within the rows of the men and women who circumambulate the House in the greater and minor pilgrimages, fully facing the faces of women and demanding them to don the face-veil in violation of the position of the vast majority of the Ulema that it is obligatory to uncover the face when accomplishing this rite.

## 28.	Terrorising Muslims inside the Haram

You do not object to those who terrorise the Muslims who are in the Meccan Sanctuary and investigate them, arresting them if they do not produce residency papers, in violation of the saying of Allah: **and whosoever enters it is safe** (3:97). In addition, these doings create commotions and spoil the climate of purity, peace, quiet, and dignity **for those who meditate therein and those who bow down and prostrate themselves** (2:125).

29. Willfully Creating Unlawful Situations

You adamantly decline to ratify, in the Islamic law courts, the contracts of marriage and nikâh between Muslim men and women for any foreign Muslim male and female if the man is a visitor and does not possess a document of permanent residency. This is an innovation and injustice for which you are entirely accountable if the man commits an illicit act.

30. Doctrinal Inquisition of Students

You will not enlist any student into undergraduate and graduate studies without first examining him in what you term "correct doctrine," not contenting yourselves with the fact that one is a Muslim from the ranks of the common Muslims who declare Oneness for Allah. This is despicable fanaticism.

31. Libeling Ulema Who Disagree with You

When someone disagrees with you over any issue in jurisprudence or doctrine, you publish a book reviling him, declaring him an innovator or an idolator without granting him his right to defend nor justify himself against such charges, as has happened with al-Maliki, Abu Ghudda, al-Sabuni, and others.

32. Attempting to Close Down al-Baqi‘

You strove to commit a major innovation in which none preceded you, not even those who adhered to your doctrines and methods before you: striving to close down the noble Baqi‘ cemetery, prevent burial in it, and redirect the burial of the new dead to another spot "far from the place of idolatry and innovations," as you put it, so as to stop people from entering al-Baqi' and visiting whoever is in it of the Prophetic relatives, the Companions, the Successors, and the rest of the Righteous. Allah brought your endeavours to nought, causing someone to inform King Fahd, the Custodian of the Two Sanctuaries, of this plan. Whereupon he rejected what you were planning and ordered that al-Baqi' be enlarged so as to eliminate your pretext that it became too full to accommodate more Muslim burials.

33.   Replacing Khadija's House with Latrines

You approved, without the least objection, the razing of the house of Khadijat al-Kubra – Allah be well-pleased with her! – the Mother of the believers and First Beloved of the Messenger of the Lord of the worlds – Allah bless and greet him and his Family. That place is the spot where the Revelation descended upon him for the first time from the Lord of Might and Majesty. You did not raise a peep when this destruction occurred, satisfied that washrooms and latrines took its place! Where is fear of Allah? Where is shame before his most noble Messenger?

34.   Eradicating the House of his Mawlid ﷺ

You tried and continue to try – as if it were your goal in life – to destroy the last remnant of the historical vestiges of the Messenger of Allah ﷺ, namely the noble place where he was born. This house was razed then changed into a cattle market, then some pious people used ruse to transform it into a library which became "Maktabat Makka al-Mukarrama." You began to pry at that place with evil stares and vengeful threats, trying to entrap it with the official departments. You openly requested that it be destroyed and have shown hostility to the authorities, pressing them hard to effect such destruction **after the decision taken to that effect by the organisation of your major scholars a few years ago.** I have an explicit taped recording of this decision. But the Custodian of the Two Sanctuaries, King Fahd – the prudent and wise man who is aware of next-worldly consequences – ignored your request and froze it indefinitely. Alas, for shame! Such disrespect and disloyalty against this noble Prophet ﷺ by whom Allah brought us out and yourselves and your ancestors into light! What shamelessness in his presence the Day we come to drink from his blessed Basin! **Alas, woe and misery for a Sect that hates its Prophet whether in word or in deed, holding him in contempt and trying its best to eradicate his traces!** Yet Allah says to us: **Take as your place of worship the place where Ibrahim stood (to pray)** (2:125). And He said, bestowing on the Israelites the gifts of Talut, Musa, and Harun: **And their Prophet said unto them: Lo! the token of his kingdom is that there shall come to you the ark wherein is peace of reassurance from your Lord, and a remnant of that which the house of Musa and the house of Harun left behind, the angels bearing it. Lo! herein shall be a token for you if (in truth) you are believers** (2:248). The Ulema of Quranic commentary said that these vestiges consisted in the staff of Musa عليه السلام, his sandals, etc.[36] Read also, if you like, the sound and authentic hadiths that pertain to the physical and personal relics of the Prophet and the true concern of the Companions (may Allah be well pleased with them) over them as mentioned in the pages of *Sahih al-Bukhari*. There is enough evidence **for him who has a heart or gives ear with full intelligence** (50:37) and ample provision for those who think and reflect.[37]

35.   Repudiating the Hanbali School

Those that came before you were of the Hanbali *madhhab*, following and imitating the school of the Imam and Shaykh Ahmad ibn Hanbal (may Allah be well-pleased with him) beginning with Ibn Taymiyya,

---

[36] "The Beast shall come out and with her is Sulayman's seal-ring and Musa's rod..." Narrated from Abu Hurayra by Tirmidhi (*hasan gharib*) and Ahmad. [T]
[37] Cf. Shaykh H. Kabbani's Encyclopedia (4:135-156)

Ibn al-Qayyim, Ibn Rajab, Ibn 'Abd al-Hadi, Ibn Qudama al-Maqdisi, then al-Zarkashi, Mar'i ibn Yusuf, Ibn Jubayra, al-Hijawi, al-Mardawi, al-Ba'li, al-Buhuti, Ibn Muflih, finally Shaykh Muhammad ibn 'Abd al-Wahhab and sons, Mufti Muhammad ibn Ibrahim, and Ibn Humayd – may Allah have mercy on all of them. However, now you dissociate yourselves from this School, declaring that "You are Salafis."[38] Shaykh 'Abd al-'Aziz ibn Baz recently announced in an interview with the periodical *al-Majalla* that "he does not conform to nor rely on the Hanbali *madhhab* and the jurisprudence of the Hanbalis" but that you "all conform only to the Qur'an and the Sunna."

Glory to Allah Most High! And were Imam Ahmad and his brothers the other Imams not in conformity to the Qur'an and Sunna? Or have you and this Shaykh and his followers all reached the rank of *mujtahid mutlaq* and the rank of Imam in the Law – one who exerts his own personal reasoning and juridical opinion without following nor imitating whoever preceded him?! We exhort you to go ahead and say it in the open, and we seek refuge in Allah from ignorance, illusion, and deluded claims! We seek refuge from having reached the time described described by the Prophet ﷺ when he said: "Just before the Hour there shall come days in which ignorance shall descend and knowledge be lifted, and killing will abound."[39] He also said: "Truly Allah does not take away Knowledge suddenly and forcefully from His servants, but He takes it away by taking away the Ulema until none is left, at which time the people shall take for their leaders ignorant persons who will be asked questions and answer without knowledge. They shall be misguided and misguide others."[40]

---

[38] Cf. "Who and What is a Salafi?" by Shaykh Nuh Ha Mim Keller [T].
[39] Narrated from Abu Musa al-Ash'ari (may Allah be well-pleased with him) by al-Bukhari.
[40] Narrated from 'Abd Allah ibn 'Amr by al-Bukhari and Muslim, cf. similar narration from Anas in al-Bukhari.

36.   Hacks Reviling the Imams of Islam

You have allowed youngsters and immature babblers (*sufahâ'*
al-ahlâm) to attack the pious Predecessors who are the most eminent
personalities of this Community, among them the Proof of Islam, Imam
al-Ghazzali – Allah have mercy on him! You encouraged a certain Mahmud
al-Haddad to publish a book in which he claims to have gathered together
the two works of hadith-documentation – by al-'Iraqi and al-Zabidi – for
[all the narrations cited in] *Ihya' 'Ulum al-Din* and which began by
attacking Imam al-Ghazzali and accusing him of misguidance and major
aberrations! This, of course, after first attacking, through all your publishing
media, Imam Abu al-Hasan al-Ash'ari and his followers who constitute the
vast mass of the Muslims since hundreds of years and whom you have
described as "misguided and misguiding others"! (See past issues of your
periodical, *al-Buhuth al-Islamiyya*; Safar al-Hawali's *Manhaj Ahl al-Sunna
wa al-Jama'a*; and others).

I have shown the [Saudi] minister of religious endowments, Shaykh
'Abd Allah 'Abd al-Muhsin al-Turki, some of these issues myself... and
nothing changed.

37.   Outlawing Nasiha to Rulers

You narrowed then closed the door of faithful advice from the
Muslims to their rulers and those in authority among them. You gave fatwa
that whoever trespasses it commits a sin and showed enmity to such advisers.
All this when the Muslims and their rulers are in the direst need of
admonition and sincere advice towards good! May Allah send blessings and
greeting on him who said, "Religion is sincere, faithful advice. We said:
[Faithful] to whom? He replied: To Allah; to His Book; and to His
Messenger, the leaders of the Muslims, and their multitude."[41]

---

[41] Narrated from Tamim by Muslim.

38. Committing Criminal Excesses

You acted scandalised and denounced al-Khomayni, the Iranian leader, and his friends when they made the verse **The only reward of those who make war upon Allah and His messenger and strive after corruption in the land will be that they will be killed or crucified or have their hands and feet on alternate sides cut off, or will be expelled out of the land. Such will be their degradation in the world, and in the Hereafter theirs will be an awful doom** (5:33) an excuse to issue death warrants and execution orders against their adversaries. Yet you yourselves later took that same verse as an avenue to commit the same acts against your own opponents, using it to cut off the heads of inadvertent offenders among the foreigners and the helpless, even for possessing a little hashish or qat.

We neither heard that you consulted the Islamic Juridical Council (*Majma' al-Fiqh al-Islami*) located near you in Jeddah, nor that you sought out the least confirmation in the matter from other authorities such as al-Azhar or the major Ulema of the Muslims! It appears that you have studiously forgotten, in your capacity as judges, the narration of 'A'isha that the Messenger of Allah ﷺ said: "Ignore the offences of those seen to possess [good] qualities (*dhawi al-hay'āt*), except in [corporal and capital] penalties."[42]

'A'isha also related that the Prophet ﷺ said: "Stave off the penalties from the Muslims as much as you can, and if any leeway is found then release the detainee. Truly it is preferable for the ruler to pardon mistakenly than to punish mistakenly."[43] Al-Tirmidhi narrated it and said:

---

[42] Narrated by Abu Dawud, Ahmad, and others.
[43] Also narrated from 'Ali by al-Daraqutni; Abu Hurayra by Ibn Majah and Abu Ya'la; 'Abd Allah ibn 'Amr by Abu Dawud and al-Nasa'i.

"This report has been narrated from her without raising it up to the Prophet ﷺ, which is more correct." The hadith master Ibn Hajar said:

> Al-Bukhari said the most authentic narration on the chapter is Sufyan al-Thawri, from ʿAsim, from Abu Waʾil, from ʿAbd Allah ibn Masʿud who said: "Stave off the penalties by way of inconclusive evidence. Avert death from the Muslims as much as you can." The same was narrated from ʿUqba ibn ʿAmir and Muʿadh with *mawqûf* chains and ʿUmar with a *munqatiʿ mawqûf* chain.[44] Abu Muhammad ibn Hazm related it from ʿUmar in *al-Isal* with a sound *mawqûf* chain. Ibn Abi Shayba similarly narrated through Ibrahim al-Nakhaʿi from ʿUmar that the latter said: "To erroneously not apply the penalties because of inconclusive evidence is dearer to me than mistakenly applying them on the basis of inconclusive evidence." It is also in al-Harithi's *Musnad Abi Hanifa*, from Miqsam, from Ibn ʿAbbas, raised to the Prophet ﷺ.[45]

You also forgot what the Most Truthful said concerning human life: **Whosoever kills a human being for other than manslaughter or corruption in the earth, it shall be as if he had killed all mankind, and whoso saves the life of one, it shall be as if he had saved the life of all mankind. Our messengers came unto them of old with clear proofs (of the sovereignty of Allah), but afterwards lo! many of them became prodigals in the earth** (5:32).

And you forgot that the Prophet ﷺ said: "The first judgement that shall be passed among the people on the Day of Resurrection shall be

---

[44] *Mawqûf*: "Stopped." A chain arrested at the Companion-narrator without explicit attribution to the Prophet ﷺ. *Munqatiʿ*: "Cut up." A chain missing two successive links or missing only the Successor-link. [T]
[45] Ibn Hajar, *Talkhis al-Habir* (4:56).

over blood [unjustly shed]."[46] Therefore, fear Allah and do not kill a life which Allah made sacred, except in justice! And be warned of the causes for remorse and guilt the Day of Woe and Resurrection!

39. Brain-Washing Young Activists

You brain-washed gullible young men with your School and rigid opinions such as Juhayman al-'Utaybi, executed for seizing the Meccan Sanctuary with his cohort. Your teacher was his teacher and spiritual master. They used to return and refer to him as well as act upon his and al-Jaza'iri's opinions. They would roam under your sights, harassing the Muslims in the Two Sanctuaries, commanding and forbidding and strutting until their force increased, their claws grew long, and they did what they did, so they were surrounded and killed, or wounded and taken prisoner.

Then you announced that you had nothing to do with them and were innocent of their misdeeds! But their books and the publications they left behind are the best witnesses and proof to the facts. For they sated themselves full with your extremist views and became completely intoxicated with them. Still you continue on your way, without the least shame – all in the name of the Qur'an and Sunna! Therefore, fear Allah to Whom you shall return.

40. Declaring Everybody Apostate

You have declared as disbelievers the Sufis, then the Ash'aris and the Maturidis – who form the vast mass of the Muslims – then you turned to the Ikhwan, then the Tablighis, then the rest of those who make *da'wa* and the thinkers of Islam... What have you left for the Muslims besides yourselves?

[46] Narrated by Ahmad and the Six except Abu Dawud.

41.   Suppressing Sessions of Fiqh and Dhikr

You forbade and stopped all lessons except yours; all *madhâhib* except your *madhhab*; all admonitions except your admonitions. As a result there are no more gatherings of knowledge, no more sessions of admonishment, no more circles of Qur'anic readings, no more gatherings of *dhikr*. What will you say tomorrow to your Lord? When it shall be said: **And stop them, for they must be questioned** (37:24).

42.   Apostatizing the Awliyâ' and Shuhadâ'

You declared Ibn 'Arabi a disbeliever then Hujjat al-Islam al-Ghazzali. Then you declared that Hasan al-Banna' did not die as a martyr nor the martyrs of Afghanistan as "their creed was not correct as a whole, indeed, they were followers of the Hanafi School, erring, and bound for destruction." You left none but yourselves as those who are saved, forgetting the Prophet's ﷺ saying: "If anyone says, 'The people have perished,' then he perished the most."[47]

43.   The Sham(e) of Madina University

You built an university in al-Madina al-Munawwara and named it the Islamic University, near the Master of Prophets ﷺ. People and scholars then flocked to it with their cherished children and sons, rejoicing at the chance of drinking from this spring, thinking it would increase them in love and followership of their Beloved ﷺ, his dear Family, his Companions, and the Successors. But there you were, teaching them how to deprecate him and all of them! You also had the students spy on and surveil one another so as to report to you the names and activities of those you named grave-lovers (*al-qubûriyyûn*)! Namely, those who made frequent

---

[47] Narrated from Abu Hurayra by Malik, Ahmad, Muslim, al-Bukhari in *al-Adab al-Mufrad*, and Abu Dawud.

visits and salutations upon the Master of Messengers and the Mercy of Allah to the worlds so that you might wage war against them, ostracise them and expel them! You would only keep whoever became your client and obeyed you – for those alone are truthful and trusted according to you.

Whoever graduated successfully at your hands, having drunk in the gamut of your beliefs, you sent back to their countries as your representatives to sound out your warnings and announce your glad tidings that their misguided fathers and wayward nations must renew their Islam. Such graduates you pampered with lavish salaries, opening offices for them and every conceivable opportunity. As a result, dissensions and enmity flared up between them and the Ulema and pious Muslims of the generations of their fathers and past Shaykhs. Such graduates resemble time-bombs you manufactured and filled with all kinds of bad opinions of others and deep-seated contempt. This has transformed Muslim countries, especially Africa and Asia, into battle-fields of perpetual dissensions among Muslims. This condition has even spread to the Muslim countries that gained their independence from Russia only recently, all the way to Muslim minorities and communities in Europe, America, Australia, and elsewhere! To Allah is our complaint.

44.   Outdoing Ibn Taymiyya and his Friends

Neither Ibn Taymiyya, Ibn al-Qayyim, nor any of the Imams of the *Salaf* before them said that the Sufis were all polytheists. Rather, they said that among them were those who reach the level of *siddīq* – truthful saint. Look up, if you wish, the books of al-Dhahabi and Ibn Rajab, Ibn Taymiyya's *Fatawa*, Ibn al-Qayyim's *Madarij al-Salikin* and others. Yet you declare the Sufis apostate in their entirety and impute them with innovation and idolatry!

The same acts are committed by your minions and newfound pupils, the likes of 'Abd al-Rahman 'Abd al-Khaliq, Jaza'iri, Zino, Dimashqiyya, Albani, Wadi'i, and whoever sings their tune. **I ask, are these opinions of yours in conformity with the Pious Predecessors or are you full-fledged innovators who single yourselves out in all of them? Is it permissible, then, for you to say "We are Salafis," when no Salafi ever preceded you in committing such acts?!**

45. Exporting Fitna to the US and Europe

Your deep-seated illness has contaminated America and Europe. As a result disagreement flared up in the mosques and schools of the Muslims, this one following Ibn Baz and 'Uthaymin, declaring apostate the Sufis and those who make *dhikr*; that one, Ash'ari or Maturidi; the third one, Deobandi or Barelwi; etc. Each is fighting the other and forbidding *salât* behind the other as well as marriage or brotherly relations, severing the ties of Religion. I have witnessed this myself and was present when a Muslim preacher was prevented from giving *khutba* in an American mosque on the grounds that he was a Sufi, following which, a quarrel flared up among the worshippers... Repent, and repent now to Allah the Lord of the worlds Who said, **Repent unto Allah all, O believers, so that you may succeed** (24:31).

46. Waging War on Islam and the Muslims

The slaughters and terrible events presently taking place damage the reputation of Islam and play havoc with the Muslims. For example, what happened in Algeria and Egypt or in the Meccan Sanctuary is nothing but the fruit of your graduates and beliefs, and the reading of your publications, all of them built on apostatizing (*takfîr*), calling monotheists idolaters (*tashrîk*), hurling accusations of innovations (*tabdî'*), and holding the worst opinions of the Muslims. If you want to see this clearly and so that all people can see this plainly, it suffices to sift through those extremists: is there any Sufi among them, any Azhari, or Ash'ari, or follower of one of the Four *Madhâhib*? And after you set them loose you kept silent and mute, sitting back and watching instead of firmly condemning their acts. You were not of those who gave them sincere, faithful advice. I truly wonder, after this, who is the manifest corrupter?!

47.   Calling Sunnis "Jahmis" and "Mu'tazilis"

You accuse the Muslims who differ with you of being deviant Jahmis or Mu'tazilis. The truth is, you are the Jahmiyya because you agree with them in some of their doctrines and you are the Mu'tazila because you concur with them in denying sainthood and saints as well as their miraculous gifts, the life of the dead,[48] and the arbitration of reason in matters of the unseen in religious issues. It was said:

> *She flung her bane at me and slinked away.*

and also:

> *Do not blame a moral trait then display it:*
> *Shame on you if you do–great shame!*

48.   Reviving Kharijism

You adopted the practices of the Khawarij. Whenever one of the Muslims comes to you – especially students of Islamic knowledge – you begin by checking his doctrine: is it correct in your view or not? "What do you say about this? and about that? and where is Allah?" etc. This is exactly what the Khawarij would do in the past. Whenever a Muslim monotheist passed them by or came to them they investigated him. If he differed with them they killed him. As for the polytheists and the disbelievers, they showed them kindness, reciting the verse **And if anyone of the idolaters seeks your protection, then protect him so that he may hear the word**

---

[48] Hence they deny that Ibn al-Qayyim authored *al-Ruh*! [T]

of Allah; and afterward convey him to his place of safety. That is because they are a folk who know not (9:6). Shall We then treat those who have surrendered as We treat the guilty? What ails you? How foolishly you judge! (:35-36).

49.   Contempt of the Ulema

The Four *Madhâhib* had pulpits in the Meccan Sanctuary – you destroyed them[49] – and teaching chairs – you banned them. Among the last to date was that of Dr. Muhammad ibn ʿAlawi al-Maliki who succeeded his father and grandfather. But your eyes could not bear to see him there, so you accused him of misguidance and sheer disbelief in your book *al-Hiwar*. Had Allah not prompted me to defend him with my book *al-Radd al-Maniʿ* and others of the people of learning with theirs,[50] and if King Fahd, the Custodian of the Two Sanctuaries, had not interfered to protect him, he would be ancient history today.

There used to be Ulema also in the Noble Prophetic Sanctuary, teaching the Four Schools of Law. The last one was Shaykh ʿAbd al-Rahman al-Juhani al-Shafiʿi – the author of the manual *Qatf al-Thimar fi Ahkam al-Hajj wa al-Iʿtimar* – whom you prevented from teaching "until he obtain a permit from Shaykh Ibn Baz." The permit was never issued and so he was stopped from teaching.

Another was the scrupulous, erudite scholar and mufti, Shaykh ʿAbd Allah Saʿid al-Lahji al-Shafiʿi – *rahimahullâh*! One of your spies stopped him from teaching and all requests to Ibn Baz to return him to teaching failed. As a result, the students were deprived of the benefit of his valuable lessons. Before him the verifying, erudite scholar, Shaykh Ismaʿil

---

[49] These pulpits can be seen represented around the Kaʿba in pre-Wahhabi drawings and pictures of Makka. [T]
[50] Cf. above, note 13. [T]

'Uthman al-Zayn al-Shafi'i – *rahimahullâh!* – was also stopped and harassed. Allah is the One Who shall take accounts of you!

Thus was the gate of teaching in the Four Madhahib closed shut after such teaching had lived on uninterruptedly since the earliest ages of Islam – the days of the *Tâbi'în* and their Successors from the best, praised Islamic centuries and even in the time of your predecessors when they penetrated the Hijaz. Yet you gave full opportunity there to al-Jaza'iri and his ilk, such as his in-law, to repeat and shout at the top of his lungs, right next to al-Mustafa ﷺ: "The father and mother of the Prophet are in hellfire! The father and mother of the Prophet are in hellfire!" repeatedly.[51] Truly we belong to Allah and to Him is our return, there is no change nor power except with Allah, sufficient for us is Allah, and what a wonderful reliance!

All this is in the balance of your deeds and under your responsibility in the presence of our Almighty Lord, without fear nor trembling on your part before Allah Who said: **Lo! those who malign Allah and His messenger, Allah has cursed them in the world and the Hereafter and prepared for them the doom of the disdained** (33:57) and **Those who vex the messenger of Allah, for them there is a painful doom** (9:61).

50.   Recent Elimination of a Vestige

There was a vestige at the spot where the Prophet's ﷺ camel alighted in the mosque of Quba' when he emigrated to Madina, at which location was revealed the verse[52] **A place of worship which was founded upon duty to Allah from the first day is worthier that you should**

---

[51] On the parents of the Prophet ﷺ being saved see the refutation of al-Jaza'iri by 'Amrawi and Murad, *Wa'iz Ghayr Mutta'iz* ("A Heedless Admonisher"); al-Suyuti's fatwas in *Majmu' Tis' Rasa'il* and *al-Hawi li al-Fatawa*; Kabbani, *Encyclopedia* (2:143-159); and al-Barzanji, *Sadad al-Din wa Sidad al-Dayn fi Najat al-Abawayn al-Sharifayn.* [T]

[52] But see Ibrahim Rif'at Basha, *Mir'at al-Haramayn* (1:397). [T]

stand to pray therein, wherein are men who love to purify themselves. Allah loves the purifiers** (9:108). You eliminated this vestige which we used to see until recently.

51. Defacing Masjid al-Qiblatayn

There used to be, in the Mosque of the Two Qiblas, a marker indicating the old *qibla* and the abrogated direction of prayer towards the Farthest Mosque [in al-Qudus, Sham], so you eliminated it on the grounds that you consider it an innovation.

52. Razing the Gardens and Wells of the Companions (may Allah be well-pleased with them)

You eliminated the garden of the Sahabi Salman al-Farisi (may Allah be well-pleased with him) which contained a date palm-tree planted by the Prophet ﷺ and you destroyed the well of al-'Ayn al-Zarqa' near Quba' and the well of Aris – the "well of the ring."[53] You also forbade sighting of the well of Ruma which 'Uthman (may Allah be well-pleased with him) had bought from a Jew and turned into a permanent endowment for the Muslims in the way of Allah. There are many other important vestiges that were either eliminated or defaced and changed.

53. Closing the Madrasas in al-Ahsa'

Followers of the Four Schools from the population of al-Ahsa' used to have private schools for the study of each *madhhab*. You closed them down and forbade any teaching from taking place in them because,

[53] Ibn 'Umar: "The Prophet ﷺ wore a silver ring on his hand ... [that] fell in the well of Aris. (*Al-Bukhari*). See also Ibrahim Rif'at Basha, *Mir'at al-Haramayn* (1:398-399). [T]

according to you, it is impermissible to teach other than your *madhhab* in the schools for men and women under your jurisdiction. When they began to hold private tuition in their own houses you surveilled them, harassed them, besieged them, and spied on them!

Are these the acts of the righteous callers to Allah, the elite of the people of Allah, and the scrupulously Godwary servants of simple living (*zuhd*) who fear their Almighty Lord Who said: **And guard yourselves against a day in which you will be brought back to Allah. Then every soul will be paid in full that which it has earned and they will not be wronged (2:281). Do such (men) not consider that they will be raised again Unto an awful Day, The day when (all) mankind stand before the Lord of the Worlds? (83:4-6).**

54.   Razing Abu Ayyub al-Ansari's House

You wreaked destruction on the house of the great Companion Abu Ayyub al-Ansari (may Allah be well pleased with him) who hosted the Prophet – Allah bless and greet him and his Family – upon his arrival in Madina al-Munawwara before the building of his noble apartments. All the periods that preceded yours have preserved this vestige, including your immediate predecessors. But you destroyed this most noble vestige which used to be in the *qibla* of the most prayer-niche (*mihrâb*) of the noble Prophetic Mosque on the pretext that "the polytheist Muslims" derived blessings from it!!

55.   Destroying an Invaluable Library

You destroyed, near the house of Abu Ayyub al-Ansari , the library of Shaykh al-Islam ʿArif Hikmat which was filled with priceless books and manuscripts. It's fine Ottoman architecture was unique. You destroyed all of the above when it was far from the enlargement of the Sanctuary and had nothing to do with it.[54]

56. Madina Destroyed, Khaybar Preserved

You also destroyed the well of Bir Ha'[55] inside the enlargement area, leaving no trace of it nor marker indicating its former existence. The Prophet ﷺ entered it as mentioned in Sahih al-Bukhari and elsewhere. You spared none of the vestiges of al-Mustafa ﷺ and his Companions in Madina, only the Prophetic Mosque. Why did you not turn to Khaybar and other places? And is it permissible to imitate the Jews who destroy and eliminate every Islamic vestige in al-Qudus al-Sharif by erasing our own vestiges in al-Madina al-Munawwara? What have you left of our glorious heritage for future generations?!

57. Executions for Using Ruqya for Healing

Finally, you emboldened yourselves to issue rulings in the name of the pure, undefiled Law, for the killing of whoever differed with you among those who specialise in [the application of] healing [verses and supplications] (al-ruqya) and spiritual healing, naming them magicians! Nor did you distinguish between the genuine and true authorities among them and the charlatans. You reserved for yourselves the absolute right of fatwa and verdict in the matter. As a result, you shed the blood of numerous innocent people on the grounds that they are magicians whose blood is licit, ignoring the

---

[54] Shaykh Mustafa ibn al-Sayyid Ibrahim al-Basir al-Maghribi told me the entire holdings of this library was whisked off by the truckloads to a remote desert location and burnt. [T]

[55] Cf. al-Bukhari, book of *zakât*, from Anas ibn Malik (may Allah be well-pleased with him): "Abu Talha was the largest owner of datepalms among the Ansar in Madina and the dearest of all his plantations to him was Bir Ha'. It lay opposite the Mosque and the Messenger of Allah ﷺ used to enter it and drink from its water, which was fresh and sweet..." Also in Muslim, book of *zakât*.

command of Allah **that you slay not the life which Allah has made sacred, save in the course of justice** (6:151) and the statement of the Bringer of glad tidings and Warner ﷺ: "The first judgement that shall be passed among the people on the Day of Resurrection shall be over blood [unjustly shed]."[56] Therefore, stop at the limits and do not trespass bounds: leave alone whatever is of undecisive status. Beware the Day punishment shall be exacted for the embryos from their killers, **a day whereon a man will look on that which his own hands have sent before, and the disbeliever will cry: "Would that I were dust!"** (78:40). **And guard yourselves against a day in which you will be brought back to Allah. Then every soul will be paid in full what it has earned, and they will not be wronged** (2:281).

[56] See n. 46.

Epilogue

O our brothers, the Scholars of Najd!

The Saudi Arab Kingdom is dear to the heart of every Muslim. Its governors – beginning with the Custodian of the Two Sanctuaries – spend every effort in serving the guests of the Merciful such as the pilgrims of Hajj and 'Umra. However, because of your aberrant and anomalous behaviour – as I described in this booklet – all you do is hurt the governors of this developing State who have placed on your shoulders the trust of legal and religious matters. You must keep this trust faithfully. Do not mix into it your lusts and your own perceptions lest those who lie in ambush not find in this State an opportunity to argue against it, that it is inadequate and incapable of protecting the important sites and law-related affairs in the cities that contain the holiest objects of Islam.

Therefore, fear Allah with regard to your Religion and your State and your Islam and the Muslims! Show more concern in combating dispersion and distance yourselves from causing factionalism among Muslims.

I ask Allah Most High that you be among those **Who hear advice and follow the best thereof** (3:18).

Was-Salâmu 'alaykum wa Rahmatullâhi wa Barakâtuh.

Your brother,
Yusuf ibn al-Sayyid Hashim al-Rifa'i

Printed in Great Britain
by Amazon